Pew Peeves

D1104452

Pew Peeves

Compiled by Thom Schultz
Illustrations by Rand Kruback

P.O. BOX 481   LOVELAND, CO 80539

Pew Peeves

Fourth Printing

Copyright © 1982 by Thom Schultz Publications, Inc.

Library of Congress Catalog No. 82-50731

ISBN 0-936-664-07-X

All rights reserved. No part of this book may be reproduced in any manner whatsoever without written permission from the publisher, except in the case of brief quotations embodied in critical articles and reviews. For information write Group Books, P.O. Box 481, Loveland, CO 80539.

To those gifted persons who have the
ability to laugh at themselves

The church is a funny place. Where else can you find such a diverse, colorful collection of folks? We've all gathered together not because we're experts at something—but because we're imperfect. A club of self-admitted failures looking for guidance from an unseen Leader. Who ever heard of such a club?

Well, it probably shouldn't be too surprising that such a group has a few inconsistencies. And some of these little problems, when multiplied over and over, can become a bit exasperating.

This is a light-hearted collection of those little peeves. They were collected from church members all over the country. These peeves aren't here to drag down the people of the church, but to provide a good-natured chuckle. And maybe, between giggles, we can catch a glimpse of how we can move a bit closer toward becoming the people God wants us to be.

So, kick off your shoes. Unbutton your defenses. Lean back and enjoy a few laughs on us, the people of the church.

The usher who strides all the way across the front of the sanctuary, in full view of the congregation, to collect your offering—despite your frantic waving that you do not desire the plate.

9

10   People who say "jist" and "Lord" 300 times per prayer ("Lord, I jist wanna thank ya, Lord, for jist being there, Lord, when I was jist feelin' rotten, Lord . . .").

Mothers who absolutely refuse to take their children to the cry room—even when the kids drown out a passing 747.

12   The guy's digital alarm watch that goes off in the middle of the silent prayer—
      playing "Dixie."

Preachers who spray all over the first three pews.

Song leaders who appear to emulate the take-off of a Canada goose.

Services conducted in untranslated Christian jargon—leaving visitors completely bewildered.

Ushers with breath that would wither a corsage.

Preachers who still won't quit after 43 choruses of "Just As I Am."

18   People who make a real performance of coughing during the sermon.

Dumb church slogans.

Easter Sunday deacons who look like they're at a funeral.

The 15th person to sit in a 14-person pew.

Preachers who don't need a microphone—but use one anyway.

Greeters who always welcome you with a cheery "Hello, Buford!"—when your name is Bill.

Sitting between relatives with a kid who can't decide with whom he wants to sit.

Preachers who begin all their sermons on stewardship with: "Now I know you don't want to hear another sermon on stewardship, but . . ."

Choir directors who sing twice as loudly as the choir.

Too-full communion cups passed to nervous parishioners.

The lady with the bouffant hairdo who always seems to sit right in front of you.

Potluck suppers when everybody seems to bring the same thing—baked beans and gray fried chicken.

30   A preacher who uses the same old joke every three months—and it wasn't funny
the first time around.

The guy with the raunchiest voice who always seems to sing the loudest.

32 Folks who carry on a bull session during the organ prelude "meditation time."

A morning prayer so long that your neck assumes a permanent 90-degree angle.

34 People who race to their cars after the service to beat the Baptists to the local cafeteria restaurant.

Preachers who sneak their own political causes into their sermons.

People who blurt "Amen!" to every comment from the pulpit.

People whose sinus problems always seem to get acute during the silent prayer. 37

38   The guy who works all day Saturday in the yard, through the night on his car, and then comes straight to the service.

Preachers who, when they step into the pulpit, change into The Stained Glass Voice.

A long, long list of announcements in the bulletin—that the Deacon of the Day proceeds to read word-by-word to a literate congregation.

People who crinkle cellophane candy wrappers during the silent prayer.

Soloists with a Julia Child voice.

Inflated church membership rolls that continue to include people who died in the Civil War.

44   The mother who doesn't seem to notice that her infant's diapers need changing.

Preachers who insist on praying in King James language: "O thou almightieth God, wilt thou witherest we beseecheth thine . . ."

People who think they have the gift of "immaculate perception": the way they see things is surely the way God sees things.

When you're a few minutes late for church, hoping to slip into the back pew, and the usher parades you to the first pew.

Congregations that resemble a mass audition for "Night of the Living Dead."

improvisational sermons that drag on and on and on and on . . .

Elders who know only one prayer—and use it week after week after week ...

The telephone that rings and rings and rings during the service.

Little kids who have to get up and go to the bathroom nine times during the sermon.

Ushers who say, "Welcome! Is this your first time with us?"—when you've been attending that church for five years.

54   People who seem to think they're coming to a fashion show instead of church.

Ministers who delight in embarrassing newcomers: "Where's Mr. and Mrs. Bin-farb? Would you just stand up? The Binfarbs used to be Methodists. Now they know better . . ."

People who clip their nails during the service.

Hymns that set the perfect mood for a month of funerals.

Getting caught after the service by "pew blockers"—people who insist on stopping and talking with everyone nearby, causing a colossal traffic jam.

The elderly woman who douses herself every Sunday morning in pungent Essence de Lilac.

Preachers who read every word of their sermons—then blame the dozing congregation for being "spiritually ill-prepared for worship."

Visitation teams who always seem to drop by when you're in your bathrobe.

62   Singing every stanza of a 12-stanza song—when the service is already running
      20 minutes late.

People who sneeze in the communion elements, and pass them on.

Greeters with dead-fish handshakes.

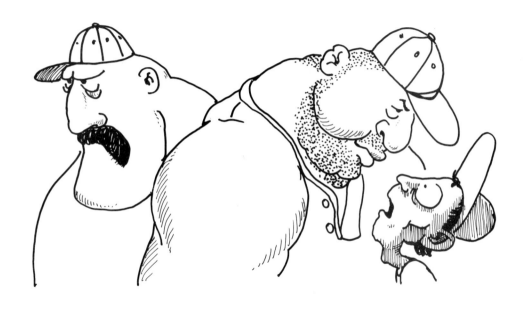

Hiring non-member mercenaries for the church softball team.

Preachers who pound the pulpit incessantly.

Ushers who pack the pews so tightly that you have to take turns breathing.

A P.A. system that intermittently picks up "Rubber Duckie," "Shady Lady" and all the other local CBers.

"Children's sermons" that take a graduate-school education to understand.

70   The lady who refuses to budge from her spot near the aisle—requiring everyone else to climb over her.

Obscure hard-to-follow hymns that were never meant to be sung in the first place.

72   "Friendship Time"—when you're forced to act cheerful with everybody within three pews.

The indiscreet church secretary: "Oh, I'm sorry, Rev. Peterson is busy. He's counseling Mr. Benson about his drinking problem."

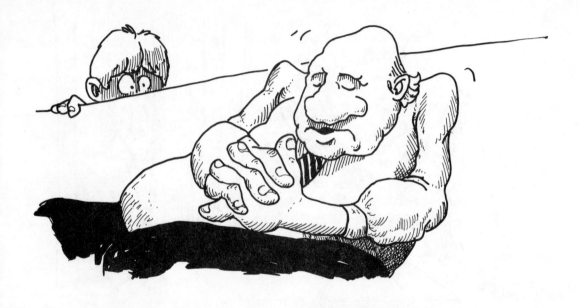

74 The guy who falls asleep during the sermon, starts snoring, then wakes up with a loud, gutteral snort.

The minister who is so hung up on his title that even his wife must call him "Pastor Miller."

The baby who, during the most solemn moment of his dedication, upchucks on the minister.

People who weigh over 300 pounds who say you shouldn't smoke because your body is a temple of God—when theirs is an amphitheater.

When a little kid plunks down on the piano during the service—and it sounds better than the organist.

People who would be so insensitive as to put all their church pet peeves in a book.

Youth Ministry Books from Group Books:

DENNIS BENSON'S CREATIVE BIBLE STUDIES, BY DENNIS C. BENSON. This huge resource offers 401 complete, creative Bible studies for ALL of Matthew, Mark, Luke, John and Acts. 660 pages. $19.95.

SPIRITUAL GROWTH IN YOUTH MINISTRY, BY J. DAVID STONE. Offers help for youth workers to grow in their relationship with God. Also offers incredible opportunities for spiritual growth in youth groups. Hardbound. $12.95.

CREATIVE WORSHIP IN YOUTH MINISTRY, BY DENNIS C. BENSON. An ideas-packed resource for youth worship in various settings—Youth Sundays,

youth group meetings, retreats and camps, many more. $11.95.

BUILDING COMMUNITY IN YOUTH GROUPS, BY DENNY RYDBERG. Offers practical guidance and workable ideas to develop a caring Christian youth group. Over 100 creative activities. $11.95.

CLOWN MINISTRY, BY FLOYD SHAFFER & PENNE SEWALL. Everything you need to know to begin a clown ministry or enhance your present ministry. Includes 30 detailed skits and more than 50 short clowning ideas. $7.95.

Available at your
Christian bookstore
or from the publisher

Group Books

P.O. BOX 481 ● LOVELAND, CO 80539